If you were a

QUADRILATERAL

by Molly Blaisdell
illustrated by Francesca Carabelli

Picture Window Books
Minneapolis, Minnesota

Editor: Jill Kalz
Designer: Lori Bye
Page Production: Melissa Kes
Art Director: Nathan Gassman
Editorial Director: Nick Healy
Creative Director: Joe Ewest
The illustrations in this book were created with watercolor and gouache.

Picture Window Books
A Capstone Imprint
1710 Roe Crest Drive
North Mankato, MN 56003
www.capstonepub.com

Copyright © 2010 by Picture Window Books
All rights reserved. No part of this book may be reproduced without written permission from the publisher. The publisher takes no responsibility for the use of any of the materials or methods described in this book, nor for the products thereof.

Library of Congress Cataloging-in-Publication Data
Blaisdell, Molly, 1964-
If you were a quadrilateral / by Molly Blaisdell ; illustrated by Francesca Carabelli.
p. cm. — (Math fun)
Includes index.
ISBN 978-1-4048-5511-3 (library binding)
ISBN 978-1-4048-5690-5 (paperback)
1. Quadrilaterals—Juvenile literature. 2. Shapes—Juvenile literature. I. Carabelli, Francesca, ill. II. Title.
QA482.B57 2010
516'.154—dc22 *2009006890*

Special thanks to our adviser for his expertise:

Stuart Farm, M.Ed., Mathematics Lecturer
University of North Dakota

Printed in the United States 6000

quadrilateral—a flat, closed figure with four straight sides

If you were a quadrilateral ...

... you would make playtime lots of fun.

If you were a quadrilateral, you would be a flat, closed figure with four sides. All your sides would be straight.

The animals love to paint.
They love painting quadrilaterals most of all.

If you were a quadrilateral, you would be a polygon with four sides.
A polygon is a closed figure with three or more straight sides.

Mariana hangs her picture on the wall.
She hopes she wins.
First prize is a new set of paints!

If you were a quadrilateral, you would have four angles.
An angle is the measurement between two sides at a corner.

The bases are loaded.
The Terrific Toucans need one more run to win!
Luiz gets ready to swing.

If you were a quadrilateral, you could be a rectangle. Each pair of opposite sides would be the same length. All your angles would be the same size.

Alice plays tennis with Ana.
Neither one of them plays well.
But they both have a blast!

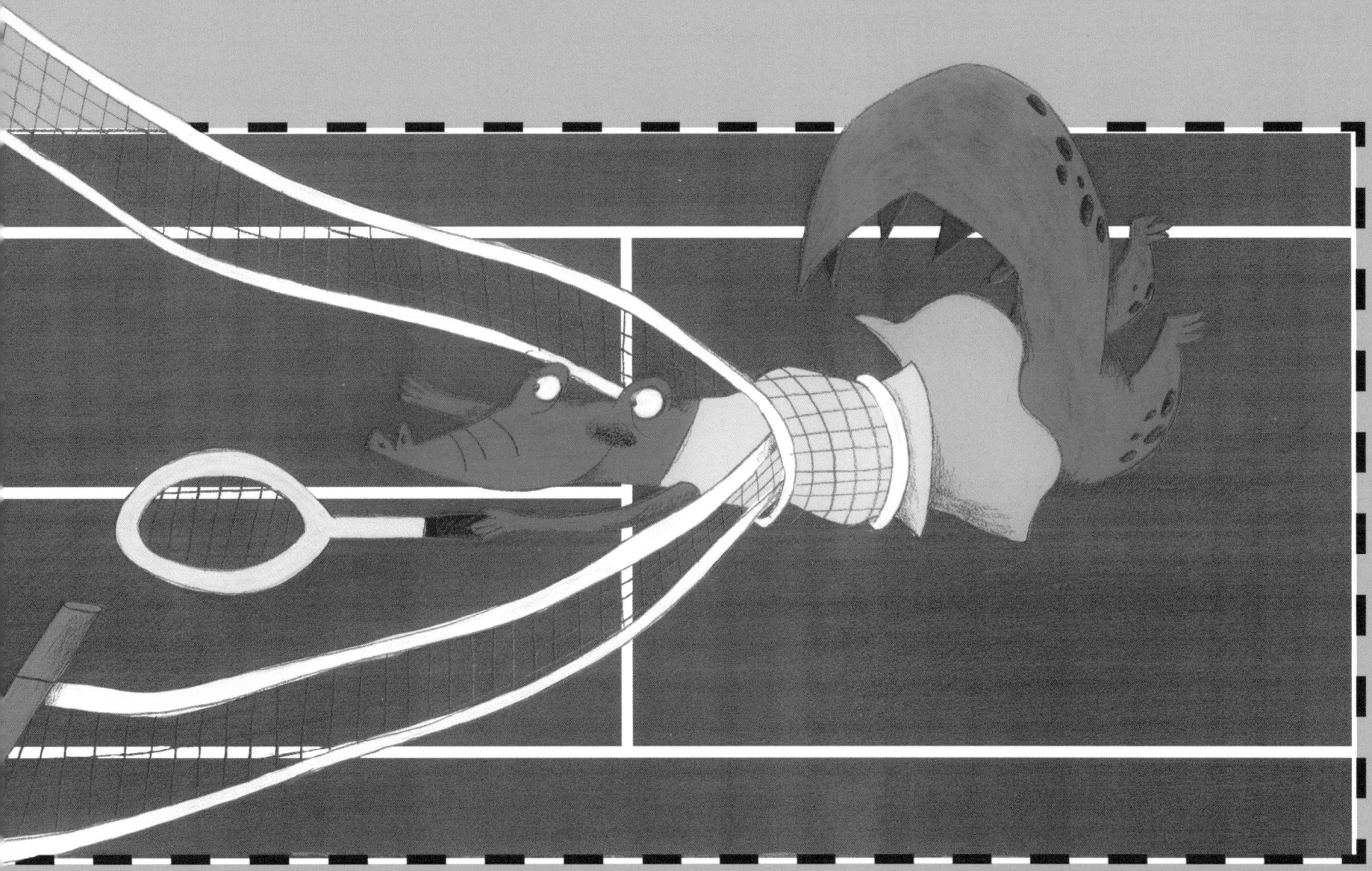

If you were a quadrilateral, you could be a square. Your sides would all be the same length. Your angles would all be the same size, too.

Bruna plays checkers with Lucas.

They place all their pieces on the black squares.

If you were a quadrilateral, you could be a rhombus. Your sides would all be the same length. Each pair of opposite angles would be the same size. A square is a type of rhombus. But rhombuses can take many shapes.

Pedro's band practices every day.

One day, the Rowdy Rhombuses will be famous!

If you were a quadrilateral, you could be part of a special family called parallelograms. Each pair of opposite sides would be the same length. The opposite sides would also never touch or cross each other. They would be parallel. Squares, rectangles, and rhombuses are all types of parallelograms.

Camila and her family work out at the gym.
They stretch, lift weights, and tumble on mats
shaped like parallelograms.

If you were a quadrilateral, you could be a trapezoid.
Only two of your sides would be parallel to one another.

Everyone grabs a kite and races up the hill.
Last one up is a rotten egg!

You could fly high in the sky ...
... if you were a quadrilateral.